BASIC STEPS
TO STARTING A SMALL
BUSINESS

This Book Takes the Guesswork Out of How to START & Make Money with a Small Business

DR. MIKEL BROWN

Basic Steps to Starting a Small Business

CJ PUBLISHING COMPANY

1208 S Sumac Dr
El Paso, TX 79925

Copyright © 2011 by Mikel Brown. All rights reserved
Printed in the United States of America

ISBN: 978-1-930388-38-3

Editorial assistance for CJC Publishing Co. by Caryn Newman
Cover design by CJC Publishing Co.

No part of this publication may be reproduced, stored in a retrieval system, or transmitted in any form or by any means, electronic, mechanical, photocopying, recording, scanning, or otherwise, except as permitted under Section 107 or 108 of the 1976 United States Copyright Act, without the prior written permission of the Published. Requests to the Publisher for permission should be addreded to the Permissions Department, CJC Publishing, 1208 Sumac Drive. El Paso, TX 79925, 915-595-137, fax 915-595-1493, or e-mail permcoordinator@cjcpublishing.com.

Limit of Liability/Disclaimer of Warranty: While the publisher and author have used their best efforts in preparing this book, they make no representation or warranties with respect to the accuracy or completeness of the contents of this book and specifically disclaim any implied guarantees. The advice and strategies contained herein may not be suitable for every situation. Neither the publisher nor author shall be liable for any outcome concerning ones finances or business, included but not limited to special, incidental, consequential, or other damages.

Table of Content

Get Started Now! 5

Simple Steps Makes Big Profits 9

Step By Step 15

Change Your Attitude About Money 29

Start Where Others Stopped 35

The Threshold of Launch 45

Get Started Now!

ARE YOU SECRETLY AFRAID OF LOSING your job and being unprepared for a failing economy? Are you ready for the great opportunities that this struggling economy will produce to make you wealthy and secure? Many people have learned how to take advantage of this uncertain economy and have become financially secure. Although nothing is guaranteed, one thing is. People will continue to make money despite the financial condition of society.

The chances of the economy slipping into another recession have risen significantly, and forecasts for economic growth and job gains over the next year have been substantially downsized. Even if the United States of America avoids a recession, as economists still expect, they seem to predict economic growth jumbling along at about 2.5% the next year, down from 3.1% in April's survey of 2011. The economy must grow well above 3% in order to cut unemployment significantly.

As a result, the economists predict the jobless rate will fall agonizingly at a snail's pace, dipping to about 8% in 12 months, not much below today's 9.1%. This trend can easily continue through mid or fall 2012. Recognizing that small businesses provide the bulk of American job growth and economic forward momentum, the Obama Administration beefed up its Small-Business Administration lending guarantee program. The aim is to help small businesses weather the storm by guaranteeing up to 90 percent of a qualifying loan and to eliminate many of the associated fees. Given the importance of small businesses to our economy, this makes sense.

It's time to stop playing the survival game. A person who lives in a country where the economy is struggling has to do more than exist, they have to make every effort to impress and thrive. To survive a brutal economy like this one, you need to spend at least as much time building your business as you do cutting costs. That means going into the offensive mode and taking action.

For those who already have small businesses, making more sales calls and developing new marketing strategies is a decent idea. However, for some of you, that won't be enough to increase your revenue fast enough. I'm talking about refining or expanding the lineup of products or services you offer, or changing the way you sell them all together. If your circumstances are sufficiently dire, I'm talking about overhauling your entire business blueprint.

Does this sound too risky? Let me tell you something, it's doing nothing that's too risky. Doing nothing gives your competitors a chance to steal your customers and your momentum. Do you want to know how to boost sales in a dispirited economy? Introduce new products or services to help your small business beat the recession in ways that cutting cost can't. In addition, add several new lines of products with a twist of up selling concepts that will dazzle your least interested client. Put your thinking caps on and think BIG. Just take baby steps to achieve your BIG ideas.

Simple Steps Makes Big Profits

IT'S NO SECRET THAT PEOPLE LIKE TO complicate the simple things of life. People have become so comfortable in operating in chaotic disorder that the simple things no longer make sense. Forget everything you've heard about why you should start a business. Rather you want to accept this reality or not, the main reason anyone wants to start a business is that many want or need more money. Let's just cut through the chase and tell it like it is. I want to be RICH, which means I have more money to do things for my family, friends, and charitable organizations.

Take your pick at an endless source of income or a skimpy supply of leftovers. They say that good things come to those who wait. However, I say the things that came to those who waited are usually the leftovers from those who picked the best from the bunch first. You can think either of the possibilities or the probabilities. No one will offer you more than what you want for yourself.

Everyone loves a gift. There is an old maxim that says, "Give a hungry man a fish and you feed him for a day. Teach that same hungry man how to fish and you feed him for a lifetime. My aim is to give you one of the greatest gifts that will help you to become amazingly functional and productive. A perfect gift for a hungry man is not a fish, but the knowledge and skills to obtain as many fishes as one may desire. Take it—it's yours! There is simply no substitute for knowledge.

You don't have to be an expert at starting a business. Nevertheless, like any baby learning to walk, the baby must first have the desire to walk. There is an innate desire in every baby to move from lying on its back to rolling over, to crawling and finally walking. Moreover, so it is with every adult, especially those who are married with children, to have an unequivocal desire to increase their revenue to enable their family to enjoy the simple pleasures of life.

My gift to you is to remove the mystique out of

starting and running a business and show you how the process that is seemingly so advanced is actually simple. You can be up and running in no time at all.

Most people who want to start their own business don't have a ton of money lying around. One of the most common questions people ask me is, "How can I get started with little or no cash?" The answer to this question is rather simple. Let me give you some simple ideas you can use that can get you started on the entrepreneurial trail.

When I talk to my protégés about business, I make no assumptions that they already know everything about business. In fact, I see them as toddlers exploring the world for the first time. So, I think of removing little obstacles that can distract them from their original intent. Have you noticed that a toddler can be crawling towards you on the floor and become totally distracted by one small object they see on the floor. With all their little mental energy, they try to pick up a tiny object that seems to demand more attention than you do. Despite how big your goals are, a person can become completely distracted by insignificant items, and miss the big picture.

Therefore, I'm making this process as painless and as simple as possible. I put together a list below of the best ideas I strongly believe in and have personally used. I hope you find them useful!

The *Four Fundamental Guiding Principles* to starting a business without much money are:

1. **Don't worry** about renting an office, hiring staff or any such thing that well established companies or small businesses have in place.

2. **Your first employee is you.** Your second employees are your family members. They can do the little things like, packaging, preparing, and loading your vehicle with products.

3. **Don't reinvent the wheel;** use the ones you have. Do not concern yourself with all the particulars like attorneys, business plan, etc. You can cross that bridge when you get there.

4. **Keep your expenses as close to one dollar as possible**. Nothing zaps the wind out of a sail like the lack of money at the beginning.

Use your money wisely. It is not about looking good; it is about making more money.

You are probably saying to yourself, "Is this it?" I believe in the KISS formula. KISS is an acronym for KEEP IT SIMPLE STUPID. You will be surprise how many wealthy business people are not as smart as most people think. They like to keep things simple. These are four basic guidelines I have used to start my businesses. Moreover, to this day, I have kept my expenses low.

The next chapter will deal with the bylaws of starting a business that you have in full throttle in just minutes. Get ready to turn your ideas into cash and create a lifetime income stream that will keep you basking in the sun.

No One will work as hard for YOU than You. Learning what to do and doing what you have learned is the quintessential to success. This book will show you how to turn your free time into learning time to make more money than ever before. It all starts with you.

IF YOU HAVE A SMART PHONE, SCAN THIS

IMAGE AND JOIN MY EXCLUSIVE VIP GROUP OF ENTREPRENEURS AND RECEIVE A COPY OF MY FREE EBOOK "YOU CAN THINK YOUR WAY TO SUCCESS."

Step By Step

IF I'M NOT MISTAKEN, YOU'RE THE KIND of person who likes to make money as easy and painless as possible. You don't want to quit your day job just yet, you simply want more income to pay off your debts, save for your children's education and enjoy the pleasures of life without having to pinch pennies. Am I correct with my assessment? This is the reason why you are holding my book in your hand because you are ready to leap into your future and eventually leave your job behind.

There is no substitute for success. Action is the one principle that has a guarantee attachment to it. When you apply yourself, you will supply yourself with the resources to live out your dream and aspirations. All true transformations are effortless. The reason why this is true is when you are pumped with information you will find your actions habitually bending to its source. You don't realize how much you've changed until someone calls your attention to it.

The baby steps state below are not in chronological order, but suggested targeted considerations to effective start your business. Together we can transform you into a MONEY-generating machine by giving you the unabridged encyclopedic sequence to start a successful small business. Do you feel the energy and excitement rising inside you? Is your faith generating an "I Can" mentality that is ready to take off any moment now? Fasten your seatbelt, we are about to lift off. Five, four, three…

BABY STEP 1

Your home is you best work place and solution for a start up business. You don't need a factory to create or store your product. Your kitchen, den, play area is the best possible solution. Este Lauder started making cosmetics in her kitchen sink, Paula White started in her kitchen, and so can you.

BABY STEP 2

Need help getting things done? Don't hire people when your profits are not realized. Use your kids and their friends when the workload is heavy and serve pizza as an incentive. Alternatively, you can do it all yourself until you have ample money coming in from the sale of your product or services.

BABY STEP 3

If you need a graphic designer to help you with designing your flyers, packaging, or advertisements, there are programs that you can use to do yourself. Teenagers are learning many of these programs at school, so it is a good idea to solicit their services.
A simpler way of doing it is using your own computer and printer for labels, flyers, etc. These are some of the programs that you can learn in no time at all, such as Corel Draw, Adobe Illustrator, and Quark...

BABY STEP 4

Unless you have a friend as an attorney and can get free legal advice, you might want to stick to the free mentoring services at Score.org. SCORE stands for Service Corps of Retired Executives, but is now "Counselors to America's Small Business".

BABY STEP 5

Your Website is your Business Card. As you build your website, it is important to have legal documents on your site for the purpose of protecting you and your business from atrocious people.

I know exactly what your concern is. You are thinking, "I thought I can get around using a lawyer?" You can by simply searching websites with a similar legal document that fits your business scenario and modify it to your needs. It is as simple as that!

BABY STEP 6

Do I need to start a sole proprietor, a corporation or an LLC, which is a limited liability corporation? An LLC is probably the best business structure, but at the beginning of making your dream come true, you need to minimize cost and stress. Incorporate later when you start consistently earning money. A sole proprietorship will suffice for the meantime. You can always incorporate later, which will be especially important in order to protect your dream and personal assets.

BABY STEP 7

One last thing before we go further into the next

phase of Baby Steps to Start a Business, we need to consider the accounting portion. Many people didn't enjoy Math in High School or College; however, that had no bearing on them when it came to counting their money.

If you have a close relative, who happens to be an accountant or has accounting skills, and is interested in helping your business by providing free services, this would be the ideal situation. If you are out of lifelines, your best bet is Excel or Quick Books. If you are unfamiliar with these, free classes are often offered at your local library or Community College. Don't complicate the process. It's not as hard as you think!

The Dynamics of Building a Website

BABY STEP 9

Think of a name for your website that will be easy to remember and that would correspond with your product of services. Let's say you are selling Weight Loss Information. A name for your site could be "droppounds.com or goodbyeweight.com. If a particular domain name is taken, don't pay a premium for a top end domain name, there are plenty of good ones left.

BABY STEP 10

Blogs is the way to go because your clients and potential clients can go to your site and get insights from your writings. Blogs are designed to provide thoughts from you, the expert, on whatever your genre or field of interest. Your blog will allow you to test out your ideas get feedback on what people like and don't like.

High school students Catherine Cook and her brother David stumbled upon a great idea for a startup in 2005. They were flipping through a school yearbook when they decided they wanted to make a digital version. The 15-and-16-year-olds got to work and pretty soon, My Yearbook was born.

In the six-year span since then, the Cook's raised $17 million in financing, attracted 70 million users to the site and generated 1.2 billion monthly page views. In 2011, a publicly traded Latino social network, announced its $100 million acquisition of MyYearbook. This is not a bad start for a couple of kids who are now millionaire young adults.

BABY STEP 11

Websites are vital to the success of your business. If you are an author, a salesperson, or have a home based business, a website is essential. You can a get a free business website at www.wordpress.com or tumblr.com. It won't be your own domain and it will read something like yourbusiness.wordpress.com. When you're ready to have your own domain, register it at domain.com or godaddy.com and add this as a custom domain to your WordPress or other free resources.

Although I mentioned two sources to purchase your domain name, these are not the only places you can do so. Google.com search engine will provide you with the other resources that are available to you. Get more incoming links to your site by creating a Squidoo page. These rank very high in the search engines for some reason!

Logo with Go Power

BABY STEP 12

A logo does not have to be a symbol of some sort. Your logo can be the way you spell your business name, which can double as your logo. For instance, your company's name can be Laura's, but its font is your logo, Laura's. You don't have to hire a fancy graphic designer to create for you what you can do yourself.

Who Needs An Merchant Account

BABY STEP 13

Accepting credit cards is no longer a difficult painstaking torturous process. Today, merchant companies have realized that they are leaving a lot of money on the table by refusing the services of people who own small home or internet businesses.

If you are going to accept credit cards when starting your business, do not trouble yourself with a full merchant account to start off. Merchant companies are too complicated, too costly with monthly feeds, and require programming.

Do you remember KISS, keep it simple stupid? Let's just keep this simple and try not complicate matters that can delay the process of increasing your income. I suggest a simpler (and much cheaper) solution like Google Checkout or PayPal. And, better yet, if you own a smart phone, you can get all the free credit processing service to delight your heart.

Here are a few credit card processing devices and services you can easily obtain by just having a bank account where the processing company can put your money. Here are just a few free credit card processing sites you can visit such as: www.squareup.com, www.phoneswipe.com, or www.paywaremobile.com. There are others free credit card processing for your smart phone. Take advantage of them and make them work for you. YOU ARE READY FOR BUSINESS!

BABY STEP 14

Having a shopping cart is good idea. The kind of shopping cart needed is base on whether to use shopping cart software or a full-blown content management system for your website. It depends on how large your site is and what kind of content you are offering. And, most importantly, which one is better for search marketing.

I would suggest you avoid the things you don't understand at this point and move to the simple and easy to understand products. If you are looking for a more professional look and a complete shopping cart at a more economical price E-Junkie is for only $5/month. It can do the job you need until you are moving a lot of products or services and need a better shopping cart system. I hope this answers your question. If you have many physical products, try a Yahoo Store, it may be what you're looking for.

Coaching and Training Is My Game

BABY STEP 15

To start a service business as a consultant, trainer, mentor or coach is not difficult. There are presently no federal regulations or professional training in place by the federal or state government to regulate this field. If you are an expert in your field and you believe you can better serve others by offering your services, why not use your expertise and get paid for at the same time?

My professional services are on several tiers of human needs. I offer consulting from business executives to marital counseling. My spectrum is broad because my experience is as such. If your strong area is in track and field, offer your services as a running coach. The field of mentoring, coaching or consulting is as wide as the ocean. In fact, it is a billion dollar a year industry.

When services are offered as a life or business coach it would be wise to develop a wordpress blog site and write about one or more of your experiences. Collect testimonials and offer your services along with your rates. Who said you couldn't become an advisor to the stars.

Select a domain name using your dominant keyword in it! If your keyword isn't a very competitive keyword, it will rank high on the first page of Google within a month or two. A keyword is a word that customers are looking in Google's search box. For example, if you are a life coach, people who are looking for one may use words like, life-coach or mentor

You Need Products

BABY STEP 16

If you are not doing affiliate programs from sites that offer them, then you have to come up with a product worth selling. You can use an eBook template like these from Eben Pagan and write about your favorite subject. It is great if you already have a couple of titles, but if not, then you're going to have to create them. Your books don't have to be long, just have content that people want to read. This is where brainstorming comes in. The key is to write about what you know. This will make it simple and easy to put out the information.

Some people write e-reports and write hundreds of articles on freelancing. One person mentioned how he has produced an eBook in as little as a day. I had the opportunity of meeting and having dinner with Dan Poynter in Washington, D.C. during a publisher's conference. Dan Poynter is a self-publishing guru who sells hundreds of e-reports and eBooks on his site, parapublishing.com. His eBooks and e-reports can range in length from one page to hundreds of pages. The prices for his items range from free to hundreds of dollars. Just to think, little overhead, no staff, but you reap tens of thousands with just a computer and your personal time.

BABY STEP 17

When it comes to writing and publishing books, a publisher is almost obsolete. A person can write a book, design the cover, and obtain an ISBN and Library of Congress Number all in the same while uploading the finished product to Amazon or Barnes and Noble, and it will be on sale the next business day.

However, many people still like the feel of having an actual book in their hands instead of an electronic Nook or Kindle. If a hard copy of your book is more important to you, you can have your book self-published at a Print On Demand printing press company. The good thing about a POD is that they will not print a single book until someone buys it, which means you have zero upfront cost for inventory.

BABY STEP 18

There are various ways you can increase your Google status or ranking. One way to accomplish this is to put a video on your website. There is a reason why video on your site will increase the probability of not only your Google ranking, but also how long someone will stay on your site.

When people use the internet to search for a product, plain text alone will not capture their attention. Text accompanied by pictures is an improvement, because the video stimulates the area of the brain that deciphers pictures. With videos added to you site, you are helping the text sink in and become more memorable. In fact, many potential customers will seek out video over plain text.

Even the most popular authors and internet gurus use video. Most of these videos look self-manufactured, and the reason they look this way is that they are. Put a homemade video explaining your product of services by using a $40 webcam or digital camera to create educational or product videos. If you use a Mac to edit your videos and you can even produce, DVD's using iMovie, which is free.

Change Your Attitude About Money

THERE ARE PEOPLE WHO SEE MAKING money as another fraud or way to swindle people out of their hard-earned money. Yet, these same people go to work for eight hours a day, five days a week; and actually work less time than what shows on their timecard. The way they feel about wealthy entrepreneurs is simply a reflection of how they cheat their own boss. These same people will be ready to cuss out the payroll clerk for being just a dollar short of what their pay should have been had they actually worked forty-hours a week.

Don't Work for Money

Most people who work for money are simply enslaved by their jobs. These people do not love what they do; they do it because they feel they have to. People whose money works for them are people who control their fate and master their time. Money is like a mirror. An assessment of your finances and the way you use money is a way of understanding yourself in the same way that a mirror provides a way of seeing yourself.

Money is Both a Symbol and A Reality.

Money provides choices for its possessors which otherwise would be nonexistent or unidentifiable. What we do with money—how we use it, earn it, think about it, protect it, donate it, spend it, invest it and preserve it—is nothing more than a representation for how we feel about ourselves inside. Your money represents your time, energy, and intelligence—you exchange these qualities for a wage. Money touches every part of our lives. It can affect our relationships, the way we go about our everyday activities, and our ability to make dreams reality.

Making Money is Honorable

Perhaps no one informed you that it is okay to make money. To have a business where you perform a service, or to have a product you believe in is a respectable livelihood. A person who makes money as a thief or a con artist is a coward who is too afraid to make an honest living. A person should not be penalized because they use their creativity and ingenuity to make a lot of money. It is the American way—the way of Capitalism. The total amount of money you have is not the significant item—the attitude you have about it is. Money is extremely important in our culture. In fact, in this nation, money determines how we keep score. Money may not be everything, but to not have a more than adequate supply of it to feed and clothe your family is a travesty.

George Gallup said, "In the planning stages of this global survey it was hoped that somewhere in the world a nation would be found whose people are poor but happy. We didn't find such a place."

We cannot avoid talking about money while so many people around the world have not learned how to manage it and are in desperate need of it. Money is not the solution to every problem. The only problems money can solve are money problems. However, to live a life of constant handouts from those who work to provide for their families is living off someone else's dignity.

> "Those who claim to never think of money usually need a great deal of it. I don't love money actually, but it quiets my nerves."
>
> ~ Joe Louis

Don't Pursue Money—Do What You Love Doing and Money Will Come

Find something you love to do and you will never have to work a day in your life. It is not a person's talent that that makes them wealthy; it is the treasure hidden inside that teaches them what to do with their talent. There are many talented people, who have done absolutely nothing with their ability but have complained about how life is not fair.

> "If you do something, you can change something; but if you do nothing, you can change nothing." ~ Dr. Mikel Brown

The Need for Money to Circulate

When it comes to life and business, you must understand that life is business. Twenty-four hours a day, even while you are sleeping, the wheels of life are constantly spinning and people are studying ways to get your money, rather legally or illegally. Money is called currency because of its current flow.

Money is constantly changing hands and moving from city to city, state to state, and nation to nation. The moment money stops moving, it cease to have any value. To make money in business you have to have some sense in business matters. To make money without a lot of money, you need to understand how money works.

Back of the Book Write Up

Basic Steps to Starting a Small Business is a bundle in a capsule size booklet. This book takes the guesswork out of how to start and make money with your small business. Does it sound too good to be true?

The most important step to take in starting a business is the first step. Moreover, this book is designed to hold your hand through the process while saving you the upstart expense. You won't have to cut corners because of cost, because Basic Steps to Starting a Small Business will point you in the direction of all the FREE services to help your business idea get underway.

Don't quit your day job because this business startup comprehensive booklet is filled with baby steps in how to turn your free time into cash. Your business will be just like same-day installation, without the delay.

Everything you've always want to know about starting a business with little or no cash is right in this booklet. I've taken the pain and fear away, now you add the action. WHEN YOU APPLY YOURSELF, YOU SUPPLY YOURSELF. SEE YOU AT THE TOP!

Start Where Others Stopped

STARTING A BUSINESS TODAY IS LIKE standing at the base of a mountain covered with footprints. Some trails stop halfway up, some collapse into dead ends, and some vanish into fog. Yet, if you pay attention, you'll notice something critical: many never reached the summit not because the mountain was too tall, but because discouragement was too heavy. The mountain hasn't moved—only the climbers gave up. And that's the opportunity.

The truth is this: we live in an age of abandoned dreams. There are warehouses full of unfinished inventions, cloud drives packed with half-written business plans, and countless brilliant ideas that never touched the market because someone quit. And in today's market—crowded, competitive, and oversaturated—your advantage isn't always a brand-new idea. Sometimes, it's the courage to pick up where others stopped and finish what they could not.

The Starting Line Isn't Empty

Let's get rid of the myth: the marketplace isn't too crowded. It's too undisciplined. Most businesses fail not because they weren't good but because their founders weren't consistent. Saturation is not the problem—stamina is. Imagine a street full of restaurants, and you're thinking, How can I add another one? The truth? Half of them are running on fumes, and a quarter of them are about to close. You're not competing with the crowd—you're competing with their ability to last.

That's why the first step in starting today is to outlast the noise. Success is less about who starts first and more about who stays standing when the crowd has thinned.

"The graveyard is full of million-dollar ideas. The marketplace is still waiting for a finisher."
~ Dr. Mikel Brown

The Struggles of Great Builders

Look at the giants—those who created industries, built empires, and turned impossible into everyday life. They didn't start with certainty; they started with chaos.

One faced ridicule. People laughed at the thought of mass-produced automobiles. "Too noisy, too dangerous, too ridiculous," critics said. Yet persistence turned engines into the heart of global commerce.

Another was doubted. Building a retail empire out of an online platform sounded absurd when it began. "Who would buy books without touching them first?" they asked. That same mindset missed the tidal wave of e-commerce.

Another went broke multiple times. Their dreams collapsed, but they restarted again and again because vision outweighed embarrassment. And now, their creations define entertainment itself.

Another broke the rules of an old industry. They refused to accept tradition as the limit. Instead, they reinvented how industries operated—and wealth followed.

Here's the lesson: the battles they fought—mockery, doubt, financial ruin, rejection—are the same battles you'll face. What's changed? The tools in your hands. What took them decades, you can accomplish in years because you've inherited their failures as your blueprint.

> "History doesn't repeat—it hands you the notes. What you do with them decides your destiny." ~ Dr. Mikel Brown

The Power of Picking Up Abandoned Tools

Think of innovation as a field where thousands have dropped their shovels and walked away. Some walked off because it got too hard. Some couldn't handle criticism. Others lacked patience. But the shovels are still there. The hole isn't finished. The treasure isn't uncovered. If you walk onto that field today and pick up one of those shovels, you don't need to start from scratch—you just need to keep digging.

For example: Countless health supplements never launched because entrepreneurs didn't have the patience to deal with regulations. Yet, the formula is still sitting on a shelf somewhere. Thousands of mobile apps failed not because they weren't useful but because the creators gave up before building a sustainable user base. The code still exists, waiting for someone to refine it. Local businesses close every day, not because their product was bad, but because the owner ran out of energy. Those ideas can be reborn by someone with fresh fire.

Analogy: A relay race is never won by the runner who dropped the baton. It's won by the runner who picks it up and keeps running.

The Mindset of Builders in an Oversaturated World

Think longevity, not trend. Most people chase what's hot. Builders chase what lasts. You don't need to be the first—just the one still standing when the trend settles. Solve the problem, not the noise. Every great empire began with solving a problem, not creating a spectacle. If you solve better, serve better, and sustain longer, you win.

Play the long game. While others want instant gratification, position yourself for endurance. The race isn't 100 meters; it's a marathon. Build systems, not wishes. Those who failed before you often relied on raw energy and excitement. What you need are systems, discipline, and repeatable models that make the business run even when you're tired.

> "Most people quit because they were sprinting in a marathon. Adjust your pace, and you'll outlast them all." ~ Dr. Mikel Brown

Stories of Starting Small and Finishing Big

A baker lost her job in a downturn. Instead of mourning, she began baking bread in her kitchen for neighbors. At first, she sold loaves for a few dollars. Today, she owns a regional bakery chain, supplying restaurants and grocery stores. What was her edge? She didn't invent bread. She just baked it better, with consistency, when others stopped.

A young man built a simple delivery service in a crowded city. Everyone thought it was pointless because "there are already too many couriers." But he noticed one thing others ignored: speed mattered more than price. While the market argued about cost, he focused on reliability. Years later, his logistics empire is now indispensable.

A teacher left with mountains of lesson plans turned them into an online course platform. Thousands of teachers had done the work but left it unused. She simply organized, marketed, and delivered what others abandoned. She turned waste into wealth.

> "You don't always need a new idea. Sometimes, you just need to finish someone else's unfinished business."
>
> ~ Dr. Mikel Brown

This is Your Step-by-Step Start Button:

Here are the practical steps to starting a business today, in a saturated, discouraging, and noisy world:

Find the abandoned gap. Look at what's been left unfinished. Search for products, ideas, or services that people gave up on. Opportunity hides in unfinished work. Simplify the problem. Don't start by trying to conquer an empire. Start by solving one painful problem well. Big always begins small.

Test, don't guess. Use today's tools—social media, digital surveys, small launches—to see if people care. Don't waste years wondering when you can find out in weeks. Build lean. Don't overspend. Use what you have, where you are, with what's in your hand. Most empires began with scarcity, not abundance.

Create consistency. Show up daily. Post, sell, serve, respond. Most competitors won't last three months. Your consistency will crush their inconsistency. Reinvest, don't consume. The biggest trap is spending profits on lifestyle. Reinvest into systems, staff, and scaling. The lifestyle comes later.

Stay unshakable. Discouragement is the assassin of dreams. Expect it. Fight it. Outlast it.

"The easiest way to win is to simply keep playing after others have quit." —Dr. Mikel Brown

Original Quotes to Keep You Moving

Every giant empire began as a stubborn refusal to quit. Your breakthrough is not in what you invent but in what you finish. So understand, the crowd makes noise; winners build systems. Ideas are common, but persistence is rare. That rarity is your wealth. Therefore, when others fold, fortune unfolds.

I want you to close and seal this with fire. Right now, in your city, in your industry, in your field—there are thousands of uncompleted dreams waiting for an executor. The shelf is full of unfinished stories, abandoned scripts, and half-built plans. This is your chance to stop saying "it's too crowded" and start saying "I'll outlast the crowd."

The marketplace isn't oversaturated, it's under-finished. You don't need a new idea; you need a new commitment. Don't be intimidated by the noise. Be encouraged by the silence of those who quit.

When you stand at the starting line of your dream, remember: many began but stopped. Your power is to continue. Take the baton, run your race, and finish strong.

"Success isn't about being first. It's about being the last one still running when the dust settles."
—Dr. Mikel Brown

The Threshold of Launch

THERE COMES A MOMENT WHEN IDEAS have been tested, plans written, and resources gathered. You stand at the edge, staring at the beginning of your business journey. This is the threshold of launch. It is the most dangerous stage—not because you lack potential, but because the question "Am I ready?" hovers like a storm cloud. Many never cross this threshold. They hesitate, overthink, or self-sabotage. But if you step forward with clarity, conviction, and courage, you ignite a future others only dream about.

The giants of industry—those who shaped economies, transformed industries, and built legacies—faced this same threshold. They had doubts, limitations, and overwhelming odds stacked against them. But what set them apart was not perfect readiness—it was decisive movement. They didn't wait for every condition to align; they acted, adjusted, and advanced.

One of the most underrated problems that exists right before launching a business is that many have not clarified their why. At this stage, before you launch, the first checkpoint isn't your business plan—it's your motivation. Why are you doing this? A weak "why" will collapse under pressure. A strong "why" will fuel you when every obstacle screams, "Quit now!"

> If your why is money alone, discouragement will bankrupt you.
>
> If your why is applause, criticism will silence you.
>
> If your why is purpose, nothing can derail you.

A builder doesn't lay a foundation just because concrete looks nice. They lay it because the house must stand against storms. Your "why" is that foundation. Without it, every gust of doubt will topple your resolve.

"A shallow reason cannot carry the weight of a dream." ~ Dr. Mikel Brown

Do not be afraid to commit to imperfect action. Perfection is the greatest assassin of progress. At this threshold, your mind will whisper, "Wait until everything is perfect." But the truth is that nothing is ever perfect at launch.

The great builders of history didn't start with flawless systems. They started with what they had, then improved as they grew. Cars didn't roll off the first assembly line as masterpieces. Online stores weren't sleek at their beginning. Entertainment empires didn't open their doors with billion-dollar rides. They all started small, messy, and sometimes clumsy. Your power lies not in waiting, but in adjusting on the move. You cannot steer a parked car. Movement creates direction.

"Imperfect action beats perfect hesitation every time." ~ Dr. Mikel Brown

Fortify Your Mind Against Doubt

Doubt is the border guard at the threshold of

launch. It questions your credentials, magnifies your weaknesses, and whispers lies like:

"What if you fail?"

"What will people say?"

"You're not ready."

Here's the reality: every builder heard those voices. They launched anyway.

My Strategy at this point is:

1. Name the fear. When doubt says, "You'll fail," answer: "Failure is practice for mastery."

2. Rehearse your vision. Daily affirm what you're building, why it matters, and where you're going.

3. Surround yourself with faith-filled voices. Remove critics from your inner circle at launch. You need fuel, not fire extinguishers.

"Doubt is loudest at the gate of destiny. Walk through anyway." ~ Dr. Mikel Brown

Embrace the Discipline of Decisiveness

The difference between dreamers and doers is decision. At this stage, you must commit. Half-heartedness is deadly. When you waver, momentum evaporates.

The great builders didn't dance with indecision, they calculated, then moved. They didn't wait for consensus, they made decisions, took responsibility, and adapted when needed.

Analogy: A rocket must burn fuel before it lifts. Hesitation wastes time; decisiveness creates lift.

My Personal Practical Checkpoint Questions:

Have I tested my product/service enough to know it solves a real problem?

Do I have a clear, simple offer to launch with?

Am I willing to adjust quickly based on feedback?

If yes, then move. If no, refine swiftly—but don't linger. Just because you discovered a issue to refine, it was simply because you defined the possible probability. Indecision is the slowest form of failure.

Build Your Launch Team

At the threshold, you need allies. No empire was built alone. Even the most visionary leaders had partners, teams, and advisors. Surround yourself with three categories:

1. Encouragers – People who fuel your confidence when doubt attacks.

2. Executors – People who help turn vision into tasks.

3. Experts – People who know what you don't.

These are the legs to your vision. You don't need a massive team to launch, but you do need at least one or two people who believe in you and can carry the weight with you.

A single flame is fragile, but a fire built with multiple logs endures wind. Your launch needs that kind of fire. Every dream needs a team, even if it's just two.

Secure Your First Win Fast

Momentum is your best friend at launch. Don't aim for

the perfect client, the biggest contract, or the grand stage. Aim for your first win. A paying customer. A signed agreement. A tangible sale. Why? Because that first win proves it's real. It builds belief. It creates confidence, and confidence compounds.

Example: A young entrepreneur launched an online design service. Instead of waiting for a corporate client, she landed a $50 logo design. That one win gave her the proof she needed. Within six months, she was servicing companies worth millions.

"The first win is not the harvest—it's the seed." ~ Dr. Mikel Brown

I have the privilege of mentoring two remarkable young prodigies, both gifted musicians, and their stories prove the undeniable power of belief and guidance.

The first came to me broken—sleeping in his car, single, broke, and frustrated with life. But in just a short time of listening, charting his course, and helping him recognize the God-given ability already inside him, something clicked. He launched his music products and services online, and the moment he got his very first customer, his joy exploded! That single sale unlocked the vision in him. What once was silence is now the sweet sound of ching-ching as momentum multiplies.

The second young man had the degrees—a graduate with a master's in music—but no clear path to turn talent into more than just a paycheck. What he couldn't see was that he was more of an entrepreneur than a classroom teacher or playing for churches. Once he shifted his belief, the flow ignited. He launched his online business, and success began to compound. His story is different because he didn't just pray and wait—he prayed, learned, and pursued. And now, his momentum is unstoppable.

This is why I say to every dreamer: learn the art of the start. Belief fuels momentum, momentum creates results, and results birth success.

Guard Yourself Against Launch Fatigue

The early days of business drains energy fast. You'll work late, spend more than you earn, and wonder if you made the right choice. Many collapse here—not because their idea was bad, but because they underestimated the energy demand.

My Personal Solution:

Schedule rest. Burnout at launch is real for those who have foolish expectations.

Manage expectations. Overnight success is mostly overnight illusion.

Celebrate small wins. Don't wait until you're rich to clap for yourself.

A marathon runner doesn't sprint at mile one. Pace yourself. Businesses don't die of starvation—they die of exhaustion. You have to rehearse the long game. The mindset of great builders was never short-term. They knew they were creating something bigger than themselves. At the threshold, remind yourself: this is not a side project; it's the seed of a legacy.

Don't launch for the applause of today. Launch for the endurance of tomorrow.

Don't measure success by first-week profits. Measure it by first-year persistence.

Don't see this as "trying an idea." See it as building a foundation.

Trying is dangerous to progression! The problem with

trying is it sounds noble, but carries hidden defeat. Saying "I'll try" gives your mind permission to quit before starting. It's effort with an exit sign. Real success demands commitment, not attempts. Replace trying with doing, and watch effort transform into achievement.

"Launch your business with legacy in mind, not just income." ~ Dr. Mikel Brown

Anchor Faith and Resilience

Obstacles will come. Delays will frustrate you. Critics will mock you. Systems will fail. But this is the price of creation. Every empire builder faced storms; they just refused to abandon ship.

These are My Personal Resilience Practices:

Expect obstacles — they're normal, not abnormal.

Treat problems as teachers, not enemies.

Anchor yourself in the faith, belief and God that persistence outlasts resistance.

"Obstacles aren't stop signs—they're sharpening tools." ~ Dr. Mikel Brown

NOW (No Opportunities Wasted), Set Your Launch Date:

A dream without a deadline is just a wish. At this threshold, you must draw a line in the sand: "On this date, I launch." Why? Because the mind will invent endless reasons to delay. A set date forces preparation, focus, and accountability.

Builders don't endlessly dig foundations. They decide, "On this date, we raise the walls." That decision creates urgency. Timelines are lines to determine the pace of your actions. You can't afford to act like you have all the time in the world, because you don't!

"A dream without a date is a dream that drifts without a rudder." ~ Dr. Mikel Brown

Mindset of the Launch-Ready Builder

1. Bold yet flexible. Move forward strongly, but stay adaptable.

2. Persistent yet patient. Push through, but don't demand instant results.

3. Visionary yet practical. Keep your eyes on the horizon while working today's tasks.

4. Decisive yet humble. Make decisions quickly, but learn from mistakes.

The Door of Destiny is Waiting on YOU!

The threshold of launch can be both terrifying and exhilarating. It's the place where dreamers step back and builders step forward. If you feel doubt pressing hard right now, take comfort—you're in the right place. Doubt always screams loudest before destiny.

Step across. Don't look back. Don't hesitate. Don't wait for perfection. Plant your feet in the soil of persistence and declare, "This is my time." The world doesn't need another abandoned dream. It needs your courage to start, your persistence to endure, and your faith to finish.

> "The only way to prove you're ready is to start." ~ Dr. Mikel Brown

About The Author

DR. MIKEL BROWN is an author, businessperson, restaurateur, and religious leader who resides in El Paso, Texas. He is a Licensed Professional Counselor with more than 40 years of experience. He has helped many people achieve success in business, marriage, personal development and peak performance.

Dr. Brown has helped people from rocky marriages to rocketing careers. His private client protégés list range from active and retired professional sports personalities to more than a hundred small business owners. He has over 14 books published, such as *When Lambs Turns Into Lions, Dream Big Start Small, Turn on Your Life, Unexpected Treasures, How to Fix Your Marriage without Using a Hammer,* and *Building Wealth from the Ground Up.*

THE POCKET MOTIVATOR BOOK SERIES

DR. MIKEL A. BROWN

Now You Can Take The Wisdom of Dr. Brown With You Wherever You Go!

GET YOUR COPIES
TODAY!

www.MikelBrown.com

www.ingramcontent.com/pod-product-compliance
Lightning Source LLC
Chambersburg PA
CBHW061805070526
44586CB00023B/2718